The sun was shining...

The sun was shining

HOW WILL YOUR STORY END?

 # Let's create a pet!

NAME

DESCRIPTION

PERSONALITY

SPECIAL SKILLS

"Time to practise dialogue!" she said.

LAUGHING, HE SAID, "

SHE REPLIED, "

"   !" HE YELLED. "

SHE WHISPERED CALMLY, "

Deep in a magical forest......

......Deep in a magical forest.

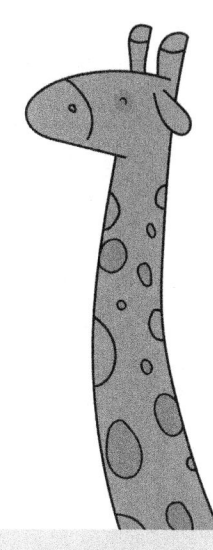

WILL YOUR STORY HAVE ANY MAGICAL CREATURES? DRAW THEM HERE.

My favourite books:

Describe two secret clubhouses.
MAKE THEM VERY DIFFERENT TO EACH OTHER.

1

2

It was a birthday like no other………

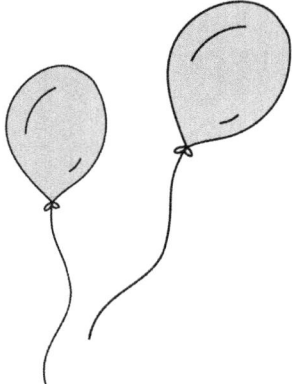

........It was a birthday like no other.

DRAW THE BEST BIRTHDAY CAKE EVER. WHAT FLAVOUR IS IT?

 Let's create a villain!

NAME

DESCRIPTION

PERSONALITY

 SPECIAL SKILLS OR SUPERPOWERS

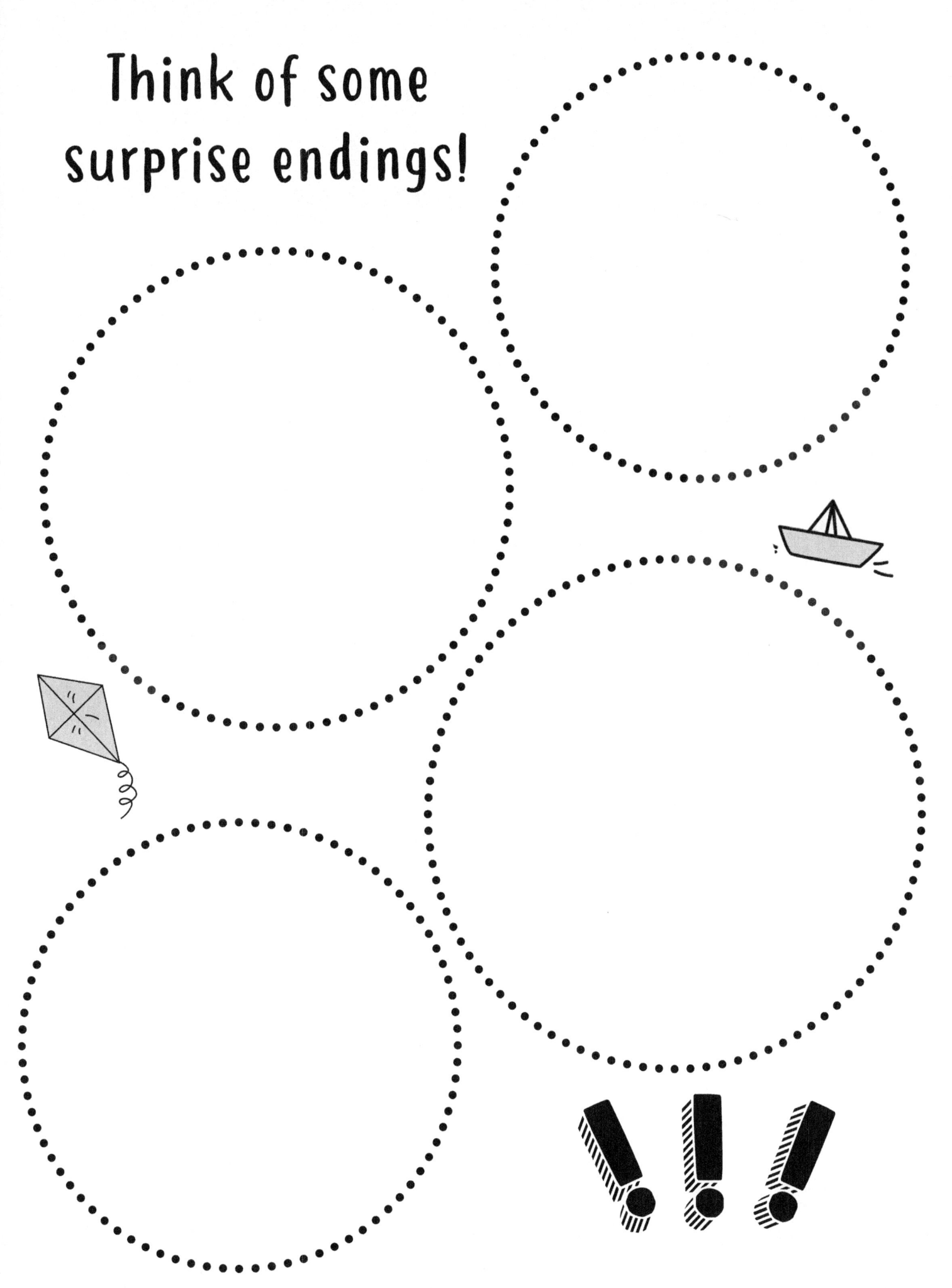

In the darkest corner of space....

WHAT PLANET WILL YOU DISCOVER? DESCRIBE IT. DRAW IT.

What makes a great character?

THINK UP SOME FEELINGS YOUR CHARACTER MIGHT HAVE.

I woke up on an island in the middle of nowhere....

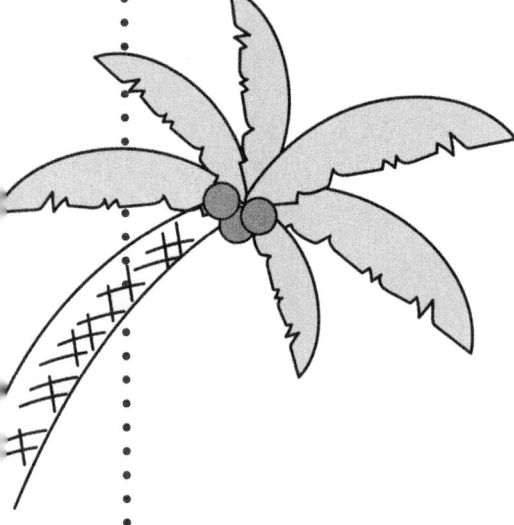

I woke up on an island in

HOW WILL YOU DRAW YOURSELF AS A CHARACTER?

⇨ Let's create a best friend! ⇦

NAME

DESCRIPTION

PERSONALITY

 **SPECIAL SKILLS**

Think of some cool character names.

There was a knock at the door........

There was a knock at the door.

DESCRIBE HOW YOU FEEL WHEN YOU HEAR THE KNOCK.

The scariest villains of all time:

WHAT MAKES A VILLAIN SCARY?

At the top of a hill stood a castle of gold...

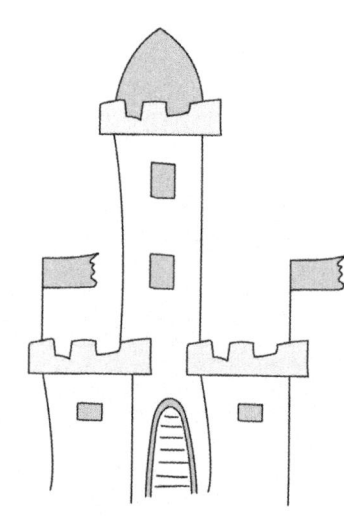

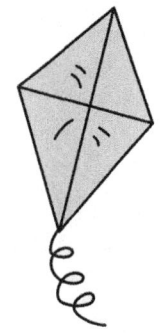

DESCRIBE WHAT THE CASTLE LOOKS LIKE. ITS SIZE, SHAPE, WINDOWS AND DOORS.

⇨ Let's create a granny! ⇦

NAME

DESCRIPTION

PERSONALITY

 **SPECIAL SKILLS**

Can you think up different ways to start a sentence?

"Who's there?" I asked....

"Who's there?" I asked....

WHERE DOES THIS STORY TAKE PLACE?
DRAW THE OPENING SCENE.

Cool ideas:

She didn't believe in ghosts but........

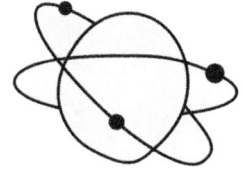

WHO ARE THE CHARACTERS IN THIS STORY? WHAT MAKES THEM UNIQUE?

➡ let's create a monster! ⬅

NAME

DESCRIPTION

PERSONALITY

 **SPECIAL SKILLS**

Let's think up some "WHAT IF?" situations to inspire our next story!

WHAT IF
DINOSAURS WERE STILL AROUND?

At the bottom of the ocean......

DRAW SOME OCEAN CREATURES.

Amazing REAL-LIFE locations for my stories:

Amazing MADE-UP locations for my stories:

One day, there was a cute puppy staring through my window...

One day, there was a cute puppy

DRAW YOUR FAVOURITE ANIMALS.

➡ Let's create a witch! ⬅

NAME

DESCRIPTION

PERSONALITY

✨ **SPECIAL SKILLS**

FAIRY TALE FRENZY!

Think of ways you can change a fairy tale into a whole different sort of story.

EXAMPLE: Cinderella decided that royal balls weren't her thing, so she went to a café with her friends instead.

The entire village was frozen in ice.....

LIST SOME WORDS THAT CAN DESCRIBE THE WEATHER.

How can I make my story suspenseful and exciting?

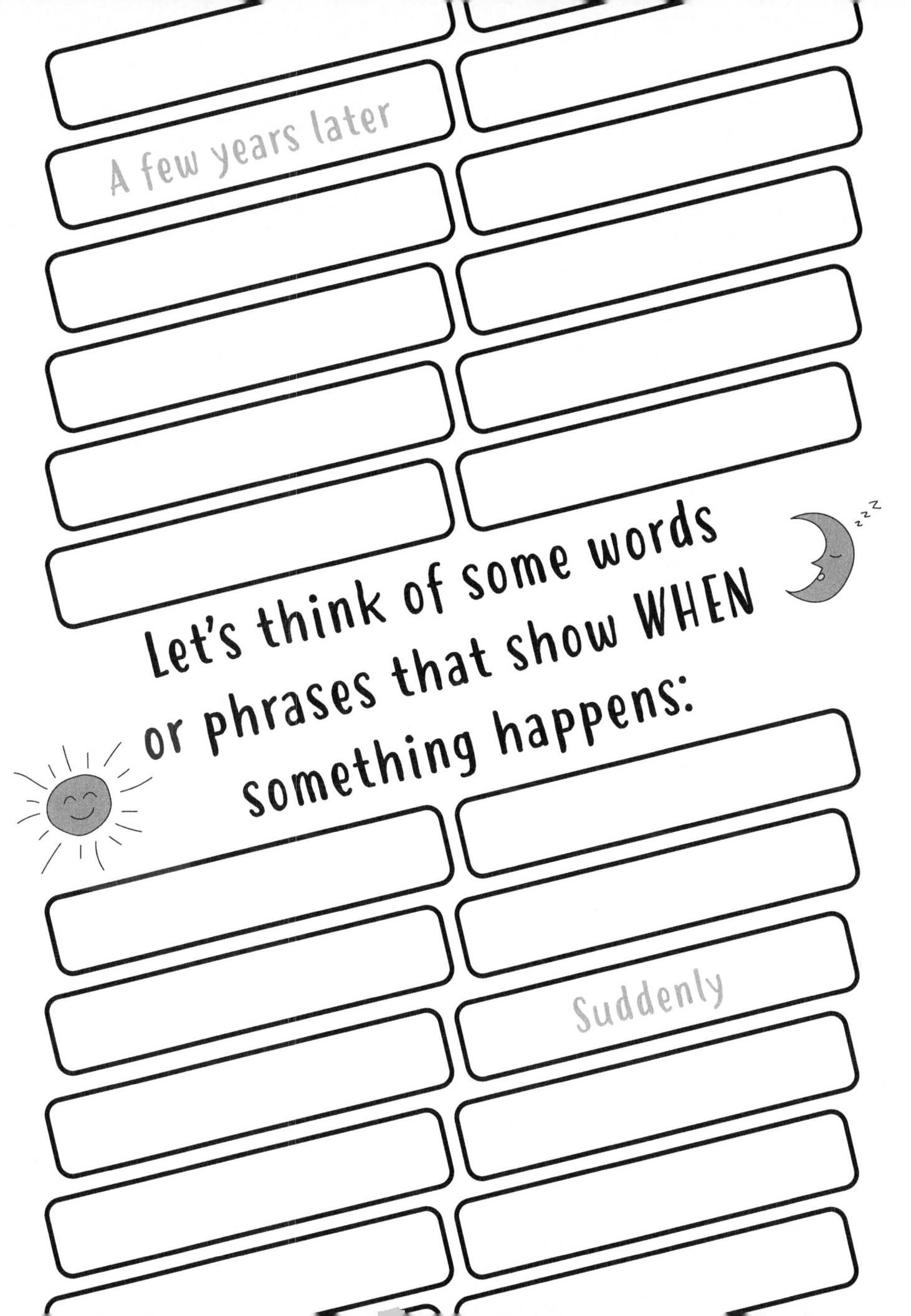

The wizard raised his wand....

CAN YOU INVENT YOUR OWN MAGIC SPELLS?

⇨ let's create a friendly alien! ⇦

NAME

DESCRIPTION

PERSONALITY

☆ **SPECIAL SKILLS**

DRAW AN ALIEN

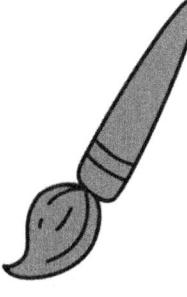

I was floating!

I was floating!

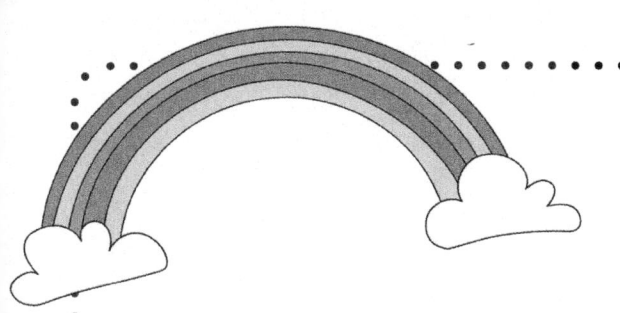

THINK ABOUT THE LOCATION FOR THIS STORY. DESCRIBE IT AND DRAW IT.

Ideas about heroes:

Ideas about villains:

It all started with a secret........

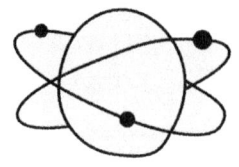

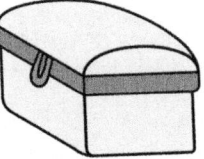

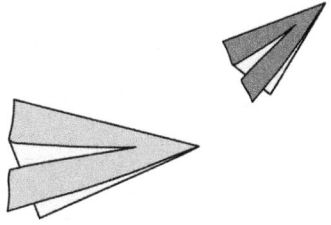

DRAW YOUR CHARACTER'S EXPRESSION WHEN THEY HEAR THE SECRET FOR THE FIRST TIME.

⇨ Let's create a talking animal! ⇦

NAME

DESCRIPTION

PERSONALITY

 **SPECIAL SKILLS**

Think of some plot twists!

Welcome to a world made of candy!

Welcome to a world made of candy!

THINK OF YOUR FAVOURITE TREATS. HOW WILL YOU USE THEM IN YOUR STORY?

Welcome to the
I CAN . . .
workbook series

ABOUT THE AUTHOR

Shari Last is a children's book author and editor. She has worked on all sorts of books – about dinosaurs, Spider-Man, LEGO, science, history and much more! She wants to encourage creative thinking and to make storytelling fun.

First published in Great Britain
in 2021 by Shari Last

Page design copyright ©2021 Shari Last
Thanks to Vecteezy.com

All rights reserved. Without limiting the rights under the copyright reserved above, no part of this publication may be reproduced, stored in or introduced into a retrieval system, or transmitted, in any form or by any means (electronic, mechanical, photocopying, recording or otherwise), without the prior written permission of the copyright owner.

ISBN: 9798520222729

www.littlepopofcolour.etsy.com

Printed in Great Britain
by Amazon